CONCERTINA

Jesse Jupiter

For my Sun

Who is my light

When all other lights go out

Humblebee

I have no words to convey my relief when it's silent and I can

Switch off from the distortion scream

Scaling every wall around me

We feel the need to talk constantly

To fill voids which we assume need filling

And I relish the behind-the-scenes string pulling,

Eases tension in me,

Assurance of an orchestra for simple transmissions

I flinch instinctively when the

Fear king-hits me

I button up my flimsy slip shirt

I push my square-cut feet

Down deep into timid flats

Tie my white trash hair into submission

Tout a white tote and forgo practicality

Notes are taken

On my general state and I'm graded

On painstaking effort

To keep up.

I let my mapped arms guide girls

Flushed and meek

Into man-made moulds

Dispense my two cents

Like tasteless Pez, expressionlessly

I'm not shy with your sex slang
Your girl things and boy things
But I forfeit, deliberate,
To maintain some privacy

I find it so strange to be
Nodding in unison
Internally policing unacceptable opinions

I'm in a constant state of high alert
I feel the static course through dormant legs
My heart ringing in its ribcaged cathedral
And my lead light eyes
Want more of the night when we laze
Legs entangled,
Stars crazed in ink skies
Burning long after sleep sets in

I couldn't be closer to anyone else
And I hold on just to hold her
When my noise drowns me out

My tombuoy, soft spoken
Till the right words swim out.

On Flowers

Cast a net much wider, engage in conversation
Bring the craters within you new visitors
To get you full on real love

Manifest your apologies
Till they feel a little less mechanical
We are a gore-geous species,
Awfully facetious
Constructing maelstroms to breed in.

But with my fevered face burnt,
With molten flesh for thighs
Where your fingers traced
Places where before only your eyes
Dared to tread
I scour away outdated feelings,
Useless now for bigger heart cavity

I still know how to start again

No fear of foolish footing on hard-won packed earth
Or of planets more established
Arms lassoed my ankles and yours
Tried to bring us flightsome, Icarusian folk down.

You and I, magenta-eyed, guided by expiry dates
Attracted to the end.

Surface Pro

I don't know how you breathe in those buttoned-down blues
With your skyscraper shoes, one in front of the other

You're another creature altogether,
Scene-stealing magnolia

But I still shivered under your hot, hot kiss
I still ached for someone better,
A reprieve from this

Just another diorama on display
Guided by an Insta-hive with
Expert cruise control

You're eating up the wordy, ghoulish, Gonzo-quoting girls
Effective with a decent script
And enough co-stars to practise it with

If you're disgraceful in the dark and they know it
Clap your hands.

Amphitheatres and the Importance of John Frusciante

You're vaudeville in cathedrals

You don't really fit

But you sound good in theory

You're the crunch of glass in a five car pile-up

You tell me all my books are becoming obsolete

I tell you you're a liar

And you never tried to read me

Scavenger, artless

I'm not the last name on your set list

But I'm leaving you synthetic heartbeats

For the four a.m. mourning

Of a long-washed-out memory

Anniversaries for adversaries

Two years post-adulation

You with your boyish arse

and green-eyed lockdown stare

It feels like the world is always sleeping

When I'm suspended from lights on poorly lit streets

I just want to sleep knowing my brain will build

Slick dream stages

Pen to paper,

Anaesthesia for selective amnesiacs

Words to make me conscious and careful

And clear.

Song 32

Excuse my eardrums burnt and bright,
attuned to drum,
Guitar and fist-fight

I'll try to absorb all the goodness
In my periphery
Grant myself love
In place
Of dispensaries.

Have Your Cake and Eat Me, Too

I assured you of my second skin

Didn't flinch when it tore

When your words got in

I scoured my arms to remove all remnants

Of anyone sleeping too close

It's easier to blend away the rot and rash

The rabble rouser

When other parts are roused from sleeping cell

And cell seeks cell and structure

Caged birds adjust their wing span

There is odd freedom

In steel bars

An awareness of space and invasion

Of the currency of time and driving against yourself

Change and remedy,

I wanted you both.

Knowledge corroded the curve in my mouth,

Downed my drink and scaled the room

For your sway

Your eyes brush the thighs of the girls you gun down

Just a little prick, then the pain

I am slowed and steadied, now

Pitch perfect in my wants

I am unmoved by the threat of proximity

And I start to want you less.

Modifier

Greenlit gene-editing practises
Innovative notion,
Cutting out dissatisfying mutations

A scalpel to inscribe on unlined foreheads
'You are problematic at best.'

Blonde hair, baby blues and her mother's
Brand new self-esteem
He's just like his father
But without the shitty metabolism
Or the inconvenience of macular degeneration

The race is on to acid wash the image of adults
Who are being told they are the first draft
Adults with eyes and noses known
By children born similarly unedited,
Not copied and pasted

Children who grow eyes and teeth just to see and digest
That they are not good enough.

That they will be phased out.

I walk past newsagents and wait for the assault
From a gamut of fake tits and lifted faces
Women screaming
Through the O of a fat lip

It becomes more obvious that our days are numbered

Our fixer-upper faces shelved

In favour of a template

Upgrades for your lowdown, good-for-nothing parts

Synthetic eyes to witness our decline

Neural pathways standardized

As we sleep through our discontinuation

Weaponized detection methods for Multiple Sclerosis

Of variations colouring the bland landscape

Of a production line

I hold my breath

Waiting for your forceps to get gutsy

To decide to sterilise between my thighs

To limit replications of me

But the thing is

I'd spare you every night terror,

Of your brain derailing,

The slow deviation from predetermined road,

From arrival at a successful station

But I do not apologize for the splits in my skin

Where gentle got in

When I tried to get out.

Gattaca nailed it with revealed myopic failing

And a faulty heart stopped my own

Imagining the reality of perfection at all costs

And the creative neutering

of unborn cultural success stories-

If *my heart's a mess, I won't admit to it.*

Patsy

Pipes cocooned in river waste
The synth and drum vacuum for the AM hustle
Hair concreted, lipsticked mouth
New routine and the skills to blend in
Like the contoured cheeks
I keep the expletives in

Blonde-bricked terraces
Gardens frayed at the edges
Cranes framing skylines we want so hard
That visual confirmation we can climb such heights
That we are progressing
A sign from sharks we are good enough.

I remember the whiskey burning my blood
Here, years before
The rumbling wagon picked me up,
Eighteen-year-old destroyer of worlds

Am I different twelve years later,
Beyond the permanence of a well-earned crease
Between my brows?
So concerned all the time over the contents
Of my wallet
When its emptiness is heavy
Like a promise

Hill View Terrace saw plenty of me
Her lights, a welcome compass
On the last train past midnight

I never felt scared with my flesh bared,
I was stealthy
Weaving in and out of trees, a steeled serpent.

There's caution tape around a skeleton gate, now
Control towers, discarded jeans
And red light cross sections

Every highway I wrote my way and wrote high on,
Keystrokes to tell folks
Where my long mantis legs roamed

I remember the cyclonic dust storm states and
The fractured roads
I disposed of.

Rust and Relativity Spirals

I'm drinking out of your five dollar veins

Your middle ground is outer rim for most folks

You come and console me

In the wake of four-thirties

Alert me to the dirt in my sockets and pores

I wrangled the truth

From every night spent hollowed out,

No doubt the sole cause

For the empty.

I find you in the strangest places

You crawl inside my glass

And I drink you down

Growl in the vice of my voice when I'm colossal

More than just a staggered, wordy ensemble

We wander the tracks late at night

Together we are devastating

I pull you out of walls,

From nothing

And build you right back up

You are the most inconsistent fuck, I feel you

And I feel you leave

You swim at the bottom of the blackest lakes

Weaving all my past mistakes into armour,

Calmer pearl you've created

Massacred bottles and bottles,

Before the sedation of routine, accidental,

Necessary.

I don't know where you came from

You never left a note

You ooze through pharma-cuticled hands

And slice through

Grey matter inhibitor alike

I can't conceive it when you're out of my reach

When I feel you down there,

Subcutaneously

You're hard-wired into every part of me,

Thankfully.

Worth

I can't begin to articulate it, the rapid slap

Of a fifth-gear heart rate

When the fever stains my cheek

When the delay in response

Makes me feel like an overturned insect

Declined, rejected, empty balance, soul crusher

Receipt of perceived shame

I blush violently

Pray for the floor

To come right up and swallow me

Just to spare me this for once

I know it is temporary

Empty wallets have never dictated how much

I adore her

How rich my blood feels when my wrist lays claim

To her fingertips

But god I want some things sometimes

I wonder if a label really cradles you,

Or feels as good on my skin

As those models keep promising

If thousand-dollar dinners will leave

A bad taste in my mouth

Just some marker, some median, some place in the middle

Somewhere we do not starve

Am I bad for craving cash-fat escapes to places only seen
In photographs?
Thousand count cotton sheets from somewhere I've never been?

I don't need the real price tag orgasm
Just some point of comparison

We grow up poor but we have so much time
We are wealthy with minutes and
Second-hand charm
And we singe our most vital second skins for a roof
To offer a brash fuck you
To the parasites
Who strive to get in

We are ragged and scarred in the least common places,
Hair stood on end
In those lit up morning stages
Expert believers and willing contenders
Fighting fair,
I watch you soar every night.

I see you,
Eyes three hundred Fahrenheit
When your mind is thick with synapse fired and I can't
Imagine you ever being average,
Dispensed on the same shelf as others
For easy consumption
My co-pilot, collaborator Rex, great-effort-expender
There is so much out there
Just begging for our fingers.

Composure

I would give anything to not have to think

about anything at all

My head is teeming with unclean thoughts

I dreamed of tallies with my formers

My sometimes bump and grinders

Up on LED lit screens in airports

When you come and leave so often it's a careful knife

All this seemingly superfluous chain mail

Linked over organs

Sometimes I need to feel wise and restrained

I baulk at the simplest, kindest hosts

In this haze

Where I climb through the walls like grenades.

I can't sleep till it's silent,

I've been using these ear plugs

Because the guy next door hacks and clutches his chest

It's hard to tell if it's a smoker's cough

Or shit luck of the draw

But I hate him regardless

For intruding on the sleep I need to find the strength

To punch him.

There are people who bleed

Up on platforms and mountains

Their hair all slicked back and nails flawless,

Skin raw and gleaming

And there are pyramids which crack

Just a little each year

Chiselled down to fine points

A red flag for bulls

And in all this time I've been one or the other

And I've torn at my wings

When some spat on their cover

My legs iron blocks and my skin just a city

If I could just sleep,

Pull you out of my chest

Hard to breathe

When my lungs get so high on disease.

Trees and a Basement Cure

With the seeds and the roots

The way that they are

I'm always shocked that I stayed so long

My leaves long dead and our gnarled foundations

We grow distorted as our recollections

They say once you've left it's not right to go back

(You'll grow fond of the hum of a railroad track)

Your limbs get talked into contortion shows

We both got too heavy for eggshells and minefields

And our need to be heard was louder than drums

So, I got ready to get gone

Lacing my boots and packing my books

I've lived with less every time I've left

To find new rooms to get close to somebody

To brave a late-night-skirmish,

And be relieved when they left

Gave it some fuel and gave it some time

Maybe I'll let someone win this time

If I find their roots in someone else

I'll get smarter

If I hear them talk too often in past tense

I'll know they aren't present enough

Give you a miss, now

Even when I missed you, sometimes

Late at night when I got hazy and the bed felt emptier

Than I'm used to

The posts I let you nail me to

You're not my S.O.S.
And I won't be still, in line

'Course you couldn't tell
From all the other times.

Contours and Whiskey In The Blood

I don't know how I find these complicated webs
Spun by the same seemingly layered
Rip-off merchants
It's fine, you're fine

When it's done and dusted
I trace the places
Over parts of me where faces laid
Complacent, coveting reprieve
From the spaces left
By dead-headed others

For all my forward thinking I'm still fifty years too late
My feet outside the boundary lines
My arms inside cathedrals

And I don't know where I fit
Along the Richter scale
But it gets more crystal every time I miss
The signs
That others never really seem to struggle with.

I didn't know how to safely
Navigate the places I gravitate toward
I grieved my losses one by one,
Of wearing short sleeves
Without offending someone

Or the expectation that the reason I'm different
Will be issued promptly,

Without vulnerability or a hammering heart.

I got close to ones I thought were like me,
While they were oppositting right against me

I pulled them down from the highest shelves
And with a microscope, examined them
More closely,
Such relief to find
A chemical thing only.

Here is everything that I have tried to say to you
When my fire was out.

Bigger Boat

Am I part of the system or is the system part of me?
My number in the line, my racing stripes,
My signature stance
If I'm a cog I should feel my place,
The steely grease in the grind-set

I'm a middleman and a ratchet girl
Ever patiently unwinding the screws
The bolts which hold us all together,
We're useful with the right tools

There's nothing we won't do.

Jack of few trades and master of less, I'm working
With your blueprint here
To make you come apart at the seams

Some rouse organs made from steel,
Devoid of memory chip
I'll keep my tongue behind my teeth
And activate my safety switch.

If I Move

If I move when I am breathing I don't mean to,
I try not to
But I feel you
And the exaggerated heartbeat which betrays me
Is a part, too of the side effects we're prone to
With all our unsteady
Who am I to hold you, really?

We're all Saturdazed and opal-eyed
Girls aligned with doorways, ciga-retinas
Slow burn for low lights

And it feels so damn heavy when it falls
a little breakthrough,
The near-kiss state and imagined preview
Set to crush, to annihilate
And we want to but we're scared
A wordless need to let it be.

The hardest part is being near you
When you're spinning off your axis
You've worn it all down and your ribs are rusted
I grew accustomed to your drowning phase

It's been years
And I try to disconnect unsuccessfully
And I'm ever more in tune to
All the devils
Taking refuge in your head
It must get deafening
But I'm sensitive to noise

The fractured thought process you cling to

As you retell the same stories

About the same people

Where did I negate sure footing?

Half-sworn promises, unending

Depending on the mood you're in.

If you're leaving do it suddenly

No lingering, no well-timed maybe

Sour The Cherry

I love a real good dirty joke
I never tell them right
I'm pouring all my wit into it and
My girlish hips align,
Obey the jeans and curve accordingly

My apprehension is misread
And paints me as a voyeur
Sudden urgent scan for exit route
From hip-on-hip and small talk

Love never served me right

I caved before the sun shot high and I looked back,
Halfway-gone
I'm always somewhere in between
The pull and push,
The mob mentality

So long to yesterdaze
We're honey-eyed on little vial
The ripest spoiled by the sun

I remember how your eyes flashed bright
Your gaze infused with
Curiosity, when you got all citied out
You cried,
'I have no heart for this.'

Your straight-set smile, your fortress parts

Ajar for fleeting second

I breathe in that jasmine smell when I walk

to work in the morning

My feet find paths amongst the trees

I hold my hands over my eyes

and feel the burn in my thighs

You're here when you're not and it's hard

To just stop

To think clearly

With those eyes travelling down me.

Cable Corrosive

Porous, dulled to mute,
Exceed all expectations
I'm foreign and born at thirteen
Canvases bled through walls surrounding
Slammed doors built for breaking skin
Music; tendon reconnector
When your skies blazed burnt,
Immersed ourselves in fragmented memory

Futile attempts to join jet engines
We were stuck, right in the middle of you
Marionettes over canyons
Legs built to last

I saw people hoard admirers for accessible feelings
I learned that if you're broken it's intriguing
Thrilling to bathe in the glow of your projector screens
We are not mysterious
We are just confused and distracted by routine

Dipped our toes in clarity and jumped right in
Both feet in for fight and a flight plan
Execute effortlessly enough
To fool familiar eyes and vessels for anger
All our sentimental recollections
Differ more than most

I came up from the inside,
Brazen, recondite
You were fighting for air

She pulled the noose tight

Guttered dreams at your feet

Like dropped cigarettes

I considered your losses

They've always held you back

Sanity seems like a complex,

A dissection

A filtered idea

Bound to lose all its colour

We love hard and collided

And we learned to drive faster

Crashing into each other

For a year

Then we learned to feign indifference

The danger of our symbiosis

Evident in shrinking frames

It's a losing game, up the stakes and

get a little bolder when

old love beckons with finger

And you come

Like a dog

And collapse

Collect your clothes from the warzone,

Slick bedrooms lined with

Friday nights spread over weeks

Unapologetically, haphazardly

We are all the world for intensely focused,

Latched-on, histrionic missiles

And they devastate the homes we build

I want the connection but I don't want to need

I run till my legs burn

I scream till the chords break

I care less about aesthetics and the adopted self-image

Was a sucker for a looker

But it stopped when you waxed lyrical on

The honesty of illness

I tried to pay attention

I allowed for an exception

I saw your face change

A flicker for a second

Imitated empathy and then I felt

The twist in the gut and the middle

I want you to remember all that *Sixteen Stone* fever

Soundtrack for a wager

That we'd somehow last forever

But I learned to leave faster

To seek out skin and heart of futures

Feeling the internal wiring in me

In all the ways that you can't.

Morning Rituals

Hour sulky, little girl

Foetal, body prone to curl

Too reluctant to initiate movement

Reddish bag of beans, good morning.

Wake to find persistent clocks

Drumming in both ears, wake up!

Drag your body further north, fill to brim your coffee cup…

Boiling kettle, burn the toast and laugh at habits formed so long

ago, feed little mouth, chew slowly-

Little man, I love so much.

Never thought to love the mornings, suffering as Palmer notes

Was rife and nearly ate me up

Till fever shook me, warmed the bones.

Happiest with radio, the voice assures me of the lives which

Carry on

Outside my door, I've listened to your tales beyond the dusk,

The dawn

The morning light which severs bonds to previous night…

The hips which found the curves in mine,

Long gone, against some lover's thigh.

Hazelnut married to coffee bean,

My bare feet press to tiles

Beneath, socks and shoes come later

In the morn once bean's infused… breathe in sweet aroma

Close my eyes to run back to my dreams

Where arms stretched

Over vast red sand to snake round waists, cue sugar coma…

Deftly drop the teaspoon in a sink half-filled,

Abandoned hours before

Two-thirds of little unit travelling by road and air-

We wait, impatient two of twenty-five and four.

[I'll never love the morning more. x]

Anchor in Chorus

Wake up inside cocoons and fuelled by

The motivations you grow in me

To swell beyond skin and words

Scan your face for what you're trying not to say,

A charcoal canopy under which we gesticulate,

Dance around truth, exposed willingly

Reach for your hand, my instincts betray me

When I try to be so cool

This isn't fair, you've sunk all my battleships

With slap-strummed swelled

Heart parts and old school charm

I feel less like an impostor when you're close by

And it terrifies

The sixteen-times-bandaged

Perforated sides of me

I'm never on my toes for long

But I balance out so well today

Rely on my need for truth

And my accidental honesty

My eyes burn under light like this

My skin used to flight says fight for this

Intermissions from love cost me nothing

And you're there past the AM crossover somehow

I don't want to need anybody

But I laugh when you swear violently

You get so indignant

Give me shredded nerves and

Coffee-drenched conversing,

And the will to stay on course,

Compass willing.

Linchpin

I want you to care but it's like pulling teeth
You're willingly comatose,
Bed-death and breakfast...

I wake up to work out,
To feel like more than grey area
You pass out in the city's lap
Your signals crash cars.

I'll break my wrists to keep from
Reaching out to you
Your words like worms in my membranes
You're just water in my gears, now

You bleached the colour from my skin
Got to find a way to fill it back in

I'm ambushed sometimes
By unannounced, lingering
Feelings assumed dead
I misread all those bright lights
Surrounding you
But bright lights are offensive
Now I'm over twenty-three

I broke my neck every day
Just to look at you up there

You were the most convincing oasis
For anyone at all.

Polymorphous Ones

Armour sure to harm her when it hammers
In the bruises
Just wanting a little reprieve from love

You notice the lethal curve
Of the shoulder blades

So easy to be scared now, waiting
Impatiently, in impersonal rooms
Under fluorescent lights
And curious eyes
I've been hearing your voice crack in my sleep
I've been aching for noise
To sever such silence
Her arms for my own
And her hands for my throat

But I try and I try and I try to forget,
To ignore all that fire in my blood

When my body is bare and bound to the sheet,
My breath in its panicked release
Everyone thought it was sweet when
Some boy loved me
In spite of my crazy
Applauding him for the grit just to brave me

Cannonballs aimed low to take out your legs
Don't listen to me when I say I'm not dying

To be loved
For the parts I aimed to Hyde

We bring especially large tides
We are volcanoes

Give me every hurricane
Take shelter when you need it,
You take what you need
You take when you're bleeding.

Foster the Brighter

Itchy eyes and thunderous thighs

Wake up closer,

Close to rising

Sun, strokes

Amber left of the window

Cast out sadness,

Cheerful hatter

Listless till your heart is triggered

From a distance

Moving closer, arrow met

With ribs and skin and chamber

Feed the growing hunger for hearts

Engaged, resisting slumber

Careless ones with metal gears are prone to rust

To lock abruptly,

Serving no one

Lovers linger, line the streets

Each with one thing

In common with the others

They look so pretty

But their minds are sleeping

Temporary souls on a cigarette break.

Figure 8 [Regenerate, Copulate]

Hearts and pages bound in stages,

Undeveloped

Eyes find me here

Elliott Smith and First Aid Kit

Through eardrums

Harpsichords and acoustic guitars

Laced with saccharine vocals

To remind me

The world is beautiful

Figure eights and chardonnay

And long-cursed computers

Bound with gaffer tape

I'm nearly with you

And you're nearly with me

I'm repeating a line

On a sewn up wrist

Your junkie girl tendencies shone,

Ever bright

Escape as you try and avoid

As I might till it seems

We're just looking for signs thought just missed

We missed nothing but reasons to swiftly disband-

And how could we?

You're my hero and I know that I'm yours.

I walk barefoot

Till my soles cover miles

I feel my legs stretch till I'm Amazonian

Slipping out of suburbia,

From the shoes you're still jailed in

I'm serene, illuminated

While you're having heart attacks

An intermission from urgent kisses,

Bliss-stained clothing on the floor

That gypsy littered the sweetest hard verses

Through me

My grown, full-formed Elora Danan,

You're hope, you're heaven.

I Am Tetris

Morph all my pieces till glue isn't needed

Just got to keep hammering at the edges

I just need the space it takes

To make room for someone

I just need a few rock-solid walls

And the colour in a cheek

Someone decided you would be home

For nearly a year I lay unscarred

Unaware of light,

The feeling of finding someone's hand

In the dark,

Laughter or sacrifice

I left a day early and left you again

Eighteen years later

You took apart my sixth home

Peace by piece

Laid it out bare for everyone to see

My seventh home smelled of smoke

And stale bourbon

The eighth of cleaning products, paint

And stuffy beige strangers

House number nine I barricaded

Myself in every night

German wino bent on reciting shit poetry,

His undying love for my toes

And Michael Jackson.

Number ten was mine and yours alone,
By then I'd made my hips expand
To compete with my heart

I fell in love with a guillotine girl
She said jump and I cut my own chords
Then she grew tired and the thorns grew in thick
Round the chest,
And I watched her love even harder

I found some little birds to fill up the nest
But I couldn't understand them
And I couldn't teach them anything

I flew over the water and found a twin
I gave her Bowie on vinyl,
She gave me a red ringmaster's jacket
Cobalt blue-haired dandy,
Cheekbones to cut glass and
Bullets for eyes
Going through me every night

Then I found a teenaged-boyish type
In grown-up clothes
Saying grown-up things
And I knew what it felt like
To hurt by omission
I fought to want to fight
But I faltered

Then I collided with a centred, fixed planet

She pulled down the moon

And examined it with me

I felt asteroids blow apart all around us,

Four dimming planets

Snuffing out overnight

She mourned each light going out above us,

Leaving flowers interlocked

In door frames

For me

Her hands carve crows and skulls

From flesh and I watch her detect

The slightest deviations

My alignment in the up and ash grows

Steadier with each conversation,

A refraction consistent with the spaces you irradiate.

Pre-chew your food, digestive, needy

All my thoughts pre-packaged, ready

Gift me rose thorns, cliché, sexy

Be a mentor, rapids through me

It must be so sweet to collapse

My blush is gone

With the curve in my hip

Your hands are blistered

You want a reprieve

My mouth is dry

When you want a well to drink from

You sell it like a magnet

But you come off like a zero

I'm cutting off my hair

To be faster from the sheets

I'm keen to crush your ultimatums

I promise to be undetectable

You scale the wall compulsively

Inspecting arms

For a breach in security

I'm riot red,

You're cheap adhesive

Bound to nothing- ineffective

Waxing lyrical on the benefits

Of applied apathy

It must be hard to disrespect your mouth like that

You fancy yourself a puppeteer
But you feel uneven and you have no taste

Watch my legs as they elongate
You stagnate almost compulsively

Check my combat boots in passing
Forgetting you is more devastating
Than any words once mustered by me.

Oceanus

We are the new model

We are jagged, euphoric

Static, bionic, fit to ripple soul,

A chronicled

Birth to death cycle

You bleed green,

Fed to the earth

I'm unsure of your origin

Birthed under canopy

Of meteors, bright

Grown nail extenders, space-shot,

Twice surrendered

To ricocheted undercover love

Forever jealous of guitars who feel

The pressure of your fingers.

Exit Stage Left, Anti-Cardiac Theft

You were salt on my skin
Your taste sworn to memory
But you never sank in
Systematic withdrawals,
Scored you plenty

Waited for a second skin
To manifest
And the urge to belong,
To be wrong about you
And go against
The gears grounding me

Sugar, sweeter just to keep her
Bite my tongue to keep from severing
All ties to trip, fall, love
Give me honesty
But not too much

I'll learn to grieve, be gritty, enough
For the week, shy smile and
The witty exchange
A little alignment never hurt,
You're just a body
And it's lonely at the top (apparently)
But if it helps to keep you steady
I'm a mouth and you're willingly
Pinned wrists

Immerse ourselves in familiar elixir

Common syndromes

For powder keg kids

Drunk on wordy confessions,

Big grown-up thing

To love, concede defeat

Completely

Measures to convince yourself

To stay in the room

You're constant, I'm nervous

Your hands shake

When you make me coffee

Mornings swallowed by tea and talking shit

You in your clunking boots announcing

All your monumental dating fuck-ups

Me in my worn in self-esteem

Grateful for a spotlight thief.

Neptuned In, Future Sea

You're electricity and I'm fuel in the wires

I'm scorched, no pity for the girlish debris

Arms up, calci-chain, chapter written,

Spare no gritty bit

Little grain of truth,

Superfood for starving brain

Alight, interior glow to span gridlines

Time expands truly,

Your eyes heavy under lights as mine

Omit the kind of lit-fuse fever

Designed to spark riot

Give me nothing tied to sense

If sense will bring me shrinking walls

I'll pull you up when quicksand girls

Cling vice-like to parts of you

With expired apparent birth right

Didn't mean to get intrigued by the seas in you,

The blue green

Tidal wash and the wave, charismatic

I'm the rocks, push up against me

With all the weight of your words

If I wait then I wait, undeterred.

Scalene

Call for intermission and we sink beneath the torrent

Brief and bitten twice before, vice bloodborne,

Remorseless

Knees buckled and I'm subpar

For the most part, beyond sun

With the tea clutched, wiry, dexterous

Expedient ghosts for guiding voice and footstep

You feel and I feel and the truth

Eats any surface politeness

You lost momentum under strobe light and smoke

I got gun shy, kept walking

Cigarettiquette intact,

Former armour and

Reminders to be durable

Elicit outburst to subdue hurt, immaculate

Undoing of all my hard work.

Have You Tried Switching It Off And On Again?

Silent editors

Strangle typewriters

Button pushing

Finger tapping

Cellar dwelling

Thought erasers

Hair pulling siblings

Computers, ceaseless crashing

Coffee spilled on overdue bills

I run and I feel the sweat inside my shirt

Fever, virus in the blood

If you just keep running

If you just stop caring

If your heart's still beating

It's worth fighting

Isn't it?

Harness

You're nothing but a freeway

I drive all over your better intentions

Screaming blind, full tilt, wild-eyed

Hair every shade of red pummelled into resilient follicles

Half-flung out car windows in a desperate attempt

To feel the wind whip my face

I strapped myself to a car bonnet

With only windscreen wipers and the buckles on my boots

To hold it all in for the night

Door slamming

Foot grabbing

Fit-having strangers hovering beneath me

All wanting a piece to take home to hang on a wall

I'm vanilla, vacant, vanquished

I used to be blinding like fireworks

Sharper than knives and much more alert

Now I'm swimming in tar

Pushing myself further beneath the oily discomfort

It offers comfort in the hold

But it unnerves the claustrophobe

Completely, arms to pin at sides concretely

And it makes me feel less than here,

Less than whole,

Less than myself.

<alteration to the prototype; Science vs. Majestic Flight.

Dimensions are *forever opening and surrendering new lovers to others*

I'm sure I've been here more than twice before.>

Cop Your Operator, Please

Dirty talkers thinking dirty talk's the only way
To get it started
But I guess some things sound sexier than others
I don't want to call you sergeant or any other army title
I really don't want to refer to your rifle
I've gotta wash my hair every night of this week
For the rest of the year

Do not grieve an ex to excess
It was never as splendid as they'd like to impress
And your skies are not deemed endless
Because of caress offered carefully

After a hard day of feeling guilty
But not guilty enough
You are unstructured and impenetrable
Because of your iron legs
And undrunk heart
Extracurricular engagements made you smart,
Not their verbal adornments and well timed deliveries,
Attempts to one up you from the start

If you feel like they're not trying to stay
Push them out the door and keep the beer

Assume nothing
Eat everything

It's easy to assume everybody thinks like you and us

Easy to believe nobody has ever felt pain or sadness in

The same vein or intensity as you,

The idea that we could all suffer

In unison silently, maybe even one day

Unapologetically…

Relating to perfect strangers who express

Just as eloquently

How they never knew how much

One person could damage another.

Fusion Con of the End Times

We are made of water

But they still want a concrete state

We are nautical messes

Trained to heel on command

Motors scream down streets,

Sirens compete for air space

Sales go down like lead balloons

I'm glad it's quiet back here

In spite of all your noise

Aero-obliteration, banishment of subdued skies

Tape your readied compliant mouth,

Feel it reach for your eyes

It feels strange to be grateful for self-imposed limits

I don't want to be caged

But the embrace isn't terrible

The urge to be less selfish adheres itself to your back

When you duplicate,

To see yourself more clearly in another

I tend to miss her in the later hours

When my brain devours

A new subject fervently

I miss her cannon-shot humour

But I don't miss the stupors

Dancing in her to a beat

I can't nor want to keep up with

A little nostalgia for a reformed nine-to-fiver

Disguises are wiser than the overshare,
The social sinker

I'm more multifaceted than the wrist
Than noughts and crosses
The daily abolishment of habitual hibernation
My Sun for your storms,
Little force to be reckoned with.

Metallure

[part two]

All these little stolen parts
Make room for new tech-one-up shards
You keep your organs, meek and mild
I'll galvanize lungs, brain and heart.

You make some space in cluttered rooms
To separate the cranial wires
But ash is dead and glass is cracked

Little amber
Less than pretty
Poured upon twin-tempered fires.

[part one]

Much love for a former postcode
I've left and burned my bridges
Not meaning to, I've lost my heart
Amongst the debris and other broken fragments,
Exposed electrodes, no safety switch smarts

There is no rock unturned and standing still
Locks limbs and leaves me useless
I'm organising bit by bit
The things that force my flight
My departure from the safest places
Much needed now to prolong a heartbeat.

Gun of a Girl

I have never felt older than her
She scares the shit out of me,
Laced with wit and steady gaze to hold you

I sewed my eyes shut and
Shoved my hands in my pockets
Just to keep the most perfect hands from finding mine
Scorched sheets left to wither and die
Under the glare of a four AM fist

You pull at your hair, bite your lip,
Twist south, borders
For strangers to cross-stitch up your skinned knees
I see you pinch at your stomach in mirrors

The secret passages you swim in
Candled temples to hug our shoulders
We are children under self-ordained idiots
And I cannot be quiet when I'm still plagued
With riot tongues
Pushing against teeth to be heard.

I wrote for a G-rating,

For general public viewing

I never had to try and I didn't owe anything

Shallow pools to drown in, deep ravines to furnish

Skin, slick with salt and valleys

With whitewashed walls around me

My bottom lip tore a little

Between my teeth

And it felt so good

To feel anything at all.

Partial two-feet-in pursuits,

Hollow-cheeked and two-dimensional

I had nothing on the truth of your head in your hands

How I imagined you'd be

I'm less storm and sorrow

Count to ten,

Breathe you in

Exhale without permission.

Exposed, lost composure and I'm drunk

On the sun-split clouds

Before me

Highway heart and muscles taut,

Taught to brave anything

Yet still anticipating

A second stolen

I'm bound to restless nights and echoed sentiment

I noticed more than you think

Tetris parts, trade one for another

Compass, co-ordinates drawn pre-discovery,

Lean close, verbose while you're struggling

Then silent

I almost always make terrible choices.

Icarus eyes blister nebula, why

You fell, I'll never be sure

Learn to steady yourself on stronger shoulders

Two AM tears and I don't know why

The whole world is sleeping and I can't get clean.

Looper

I'm by your wayside
Your brain liquor quicker than most
To knock a host out

I want to see the sun rise
But my eyes fall involuntarily
I don't remember the last full night's sleep I've had
It's been weeks, been six months between dreams
Before the dawn breaks I'm lying here
Assured of long overdue sweet omissions
Kept locked up in computer screens

We entertain the need for tomorrows without
Former bed-dwellers
Helter-skelter girls, reminders of
Jumping through hoops

We are arrogant enough to think we have control
We are salt, we are membrane,
We are skin which tears
And organs which rupture,
The bones sure to erode over time,
Time permitting, we are fortunate.

Third Wheel

Pour my two cents and my ego into a pot and stir it

My hands calloused from the hours devoured

By shovel and chainsaw

I feed on what I find

I thieve to thrive sometimes and feel no guilt

Your giants don't lose sleep over small change

I don't lose sleep over profit margins

The alveoli strangle of a seven-day stretch

In the aisles

Beans and seeds to line your stomach,

Health in spades and holes in your pockets

I eat what I see and digest your speeches

On the value of rationed wealth,

Of divide

Forgive my lack of subscription to a system,

The awareness that it needs to happen

Is depressing enough

Even as the cogs weaken your menace

My back yields for nobody, my shoulders squared, solid

With the sun on my back I mourn sleep only briefly

The trees arch to meet me post-clock-off,

Remind me to find beauty in simplicity,

To crave the routines formerly scoffed at

I am not hardened by the weight charged to crush me

The silence of six AM stir and shuffle to scrub my face

Broken by the faucet,

Furious for my skin

I exhale a little more shallowly than I'd like

I time my steps and wring out my hair

I feel its stealth in the commando crawl

Past the blades of my shoulders

I won't break my bones for a home

I don't own

For a room I regenerate in

Only to sweep floors I sweat on

To accept what is there and take what I can get

To put a little distance between us

And the second-hand debt

Dress it up with the tax talk and the single dad folly

Nobody's hostage to a silver tongue.

Sum of it

Do not lose weight.

Lose yourself in a book, in film, in music.

Buy music. Read the liner notes.

Fall in love with the art to which people lost sweat and relationships.

Sacrifice five minutes of your day to pick out the bass, guitar and drums

In one song and hear

How they have a better marriage than all your friends.

Settle on wine or rum if you must, but

Do not settle for gaslighting motherfuckers

who

make

you

feel

small.

Do not settle for a warm body beside you

If yours stays cold.

Speak up when your gut says no

Even when your truth is hard to digest.

You are not Gaviscon in a bra

To be fed to feeble idiots

To help them sleep at night.

Be the top shelf curry with the extra, extra hot spice that keeps them

Up.

All.

Night...
Wondering how so much strength
Can be in something that looks so damn pretty.

Every time you think you are just one person and
Can't make a difference
Remind yourself how annoying a mosquito is
In the middle of forty-fucking-two-degree heat
When you just wanna lie naked but you can't
And you tell me that does not bother you.
Only female mosquitoes make that sound.

This tells me we're meant to make noise, too.

Grown

I envisioned a Tildaesque
Sweet transformation
Cheekbone stalactites
With the Bowie mutation
I hated the hips and the tits
Willed the wits to stick for the
Evolution at twelve

If I've got to get hard like the steel
Round my legs
I start with the nails grown to grip
At the rails to fence me in
The wail, fit to deafen, here's the lesson:
We are learning that university means business.

Profit off sweat and the text,
Hidden meanings
Stitch together an impressive go-getter to present
To a tutor, keep your educator closer
Get your snack box with your iPadlocks
Be a joiner with a banner
Dilute your first-year answers
Four year sentence for a year of rejection emails
Your payments, parental weight, nights sleepless
Our negative balances
One governmental drain for another
You'd better learn to sew your pockets shut
Hide your side profits in your bedside tables
Get clever, get angry
Get good at filling out forms

We are dispensable, programmed to fail if we baulk

At demands beyond fairness,

Adherence to late night shifts outside

The nine-to-five

We're greyed at twenty-two and weary,

Borrowing on credit, on credit, on credit

What a credit to society

The value of a nation of exceptional, upskilled tradies

More well-versed

In life lessons as Ivy Leaguers climbs steadily;

Self-educated out of necessity

Out of the need to eat and feed a family

Who are not starving daily enough for a subsidy.

Fortunate Sun

If a gun to my head is the lead balloon

Of your week of fat cheque feelings

You're not listening

I've got a full head and an empty wallet to

Weigh me down, down, down

My toes blistered at the edges

From the forty hours committed to a roof

Over my boy, he is oblivious

To the sleeplessness incurred by bad credit,

Never sure if direct debits would end up rejected

Exorbitant fees kept my knees

On the floor for the months

Between pay cheque and pay cheque

My arms carved from wood from the food carried home

Get it made, get him grown on the good grains,

Eat later when he's sleeping,

When I forget about the second cup of tea stirred,

My brain spent on words

Spilled all over the table

Ten thousand reasons to be strong and able

To handle the five AM hustle

The mental marathon

Run on such minimal fuel,

But it's cool,

I'm not suffering.

I try to explain I'm not game for your uppers

Nor diving through hoops
Reserved for the others
My brain just needs to access channels
To tune the static into
Some lanes built to barricade me
To keep me from freewheeling through traffic

But you see it all week
The twitchers, the skittish
You trust just to lose wars
Waged by angrier hornets
But I'll earn it, I'll keep it.

Pizza Corn Thins and You Go Alright.

Pizza Corn Thins saved my life.

Today I fought tears and entertained the notion of caving

But the challenge of holding back was compelling

Pizza Corn Thins and overly nectarous white wine,

The type which incurs an instant headache

But I needed wine and I needed sustenance and there you were,

You salty fucker.

I stomached the tide of a no return on pills

Sorely needed and the writhe and burn anticipated

Years of one thing I could count on

To abide by the description and level the tide

Of uncensored anxieties

The shit held mostly inside of me, usually

My apologies.

But you stand there beside me,

In spite of my warnings

Your teeth set for the extent of my bare-chested confessions,

Or to reset whatever parameters we set

Way back when we were a novel concept

Our noble attempts at the nine-to-five shuffle

Meshed with late night exchanges

On the floor of my kitchen

God you're something, and we're something together

Grief is easy when it doesn't get in your bones

Before cavities are claimed by first conversations

And dates you made important

You try to rehome all the unsuitably

Emotional heavy weights

Guide a girl to what she can weigh

My worth eats dollars

When you hold me to unsustainable measures

People like you

Rotting in impressive structures

Insisting you're like me

We're trained to spot investors

And poorly practised poker faces

We're gunned down by piss-poor wages

We negotiate to lower brackets

We're raised to want much better

The truth is we're told when we are young

That abuse is wrong

To speak up when we feel threatened

Then we work for men who hate women

And women who hate other women

And we say nothing

We eat our words at our desks

Get too full for food

Say thanks for the opportunity to be fucked

Out of an income

Thanks for the chance to ration my meals

Cheers for the reinforcement of long-held beliefs

The things you'll endure for a home

To crumble in.

Acid Wash and a Sunday

The silver lightning splits the ivy of my hair,

Taking up occupancy

Around the borders of new growth-strangled forests

The burn off is encouraging

I stain and cull the branches into petrified trees

And watch the grooves below bore deeper

Into the earth,

Where the roots contort

Into a nose and mouth

Which swells and ripples

And my voice becomes distorted

As the chords slacken like an unwound cassette tape

If you prised my body open you could see the years in rings

My DNA carved into the trunk

Like a promise

The splinter at the hollows warmed by eyes doused in flame

Is the mouth of splits formed, subterranean

Tectonic plates shifting to shoulder the wave

My bones resent the shrink-wrap skin

As my legs grow cumbrous

And my brain becomes dulled and unimpressive

Some days the urge to leave the sheets

Is only urgency to urinate

I nod off trying to remember where I left my glasses

Only to knee myself in the face

We never really grow beyond teenaged behaviours
We are selfish with our time and our energy
We grow to resent only the stealing of it, mostly

The bent will of you and the bent will of me,
Meeting somewhere not quite in the middle
Wherever the weight of arms is needed,
To the left or our other, other left

I took it upon myself to need to happen to someone else
To be a force of nature,
Strong as others you have felt

I tried to feed you sandwiches
And hoped you'd not detect
The shit I'd used for filling
Unimproved by condiment
Turns out that honesty goes further than some excrement.

But when my tongue is weaponized,
I stifle every blast
Behind my teeth, incisor shields
For all the words I'd blow apart
When I see you pull out shrapnel
From the blows you've dealt yourself
I'm grateful for a timed release
And suns still in the earth.

Babeslayer

One thing I learned quicker than most

Is anger is only as good as the host

Your blood burns hot and you get it all done

But you don't let your voice compete

With the sun over which falls first

My girl has her fists at her sides every day,

Her hair in her eyes

And the gun at her hip

I see her curve rest at the end of the day,

The battle fought well

And the crush and the sway

Of every line scrawled and committed

To the hotels of html check-in

After the initial nine AM sardine jam

We met at the gate and the lemon tree bent

Gave way to the blush and the eye-lock

And your patent shoes shone in the leer of the sky

Desperate to hear the choked laugh in your throat

At the awkward confessions I tried to suppress

Fighting to be heard over horns and hammered heart

I forgot what I drink and my favourite songs

The movies I'd seen and where I felt home

I swallowed my nerves in the smallest of hours

To get closer

Your sweet stutter stagger got the better of me

We drank rum with the fire and lost time to backseat

And Bellamy

A real thing for Absolution

Rot

You used to be the header for every sentence spilled
Now you're barely indexed under anything I've felt

Every new alignment up against a yardstick, true
Five years for the work of white ants,
Loyal just to you.

Zero Cool

Your displays are so distorted

You don't monitor yourself

But you're quick to pinpoint viruses

In everybody else

You call at 3 AM just to tell me

That you're high

That I really need to listen

To some song that makes you feel

A little less like dying

But you still collapse like empires

Every time you meet someone

And you go down like a lead balloon

But you think

you're

the

passionate one

But just like lightning

You've got shitty timing

You're gone in a flash

But just long enough

To lay blame for your messes to spite me

You're a bit like Rohypnol

At first undetectable

But my head becomes flooded with thoughts

Which are not mine originally

You warp my recollections till my own name

Sounds unfamiliar

Your bitter little comments peel you open finally

I see the zest is lacking

But your flesh still yearns to sting

I've sometimes felt important

Till you've felt somebody else

So many little promises

But none kept to yourself.

Munster Road Trip

A baked hill

Rubble and human debris settle in for the night

I carry Ramona in her shell and see the beacon

Blazing before me

I raise a tired arm

My tendons are spaghetti

My fingers are long numb

But they cradle her like a receiver

I wonder how many people have told you stories

And forgotten very important dates just to touch you

I'm not sure where you came from

Or who loved you first

You tell me that you've travelled to more places than I ever will

And I promise myself right now that I will prove you wrong

You're mine now.

You're beautiful and I'll be careful not to forget you

Or condemn you to the dark

Just to gather dust and be another in the line

I let my feet lead me onto ten buses,

Rumbling old fuckers

With cheerful weird fuckers on them

This eighty-year-old lady called some guy an arsehole to his face

For pushing in front of me

She made me feel excited to get really old

So I can say really offensive things

Because it's impolite to tell an old lady to go fuck herself.

I let my feet lead me onto two trains bound for cities

I watched this schizophrenic guy chastise himself

As he twitched involuntarily

I wanted to trade bodies so he could have a little peace

But maybe my cerebral carnival

Glares a bit too brightly

My head was cut-and-paste conversations

Reignited the transmission temporarily

And I was curious

To hear if they thought like me

I couldn't bring myself to abandon the house this morning

To walk one hundred metres to a bench

Without the skies suddenly seeming split apart

And much, much bigger.

I paid a girl to cut my hair and was glad it was not as dead

As I suspected, but also slightly disappointed

I didn't really need to shave

My head to save it.

I collected my prescription and washed the pills

Right down

To the well of my stomach

And felt my eyes grow sharp again

I felt my brain flicker back to life

Like a monstrous LED screen

All these little cranial wires short circuiting

One of few consistencies

I can count on with

This maladaptive frequency

The urge to merge with the rest disconcerts me

When alerts chirp to warn me

Of impending social doomscape

But I miss the interactions

When they get under my skin

When a serendipitous song choice leaves a bruise

The hard drive inside me isn't fooled by Trojan horses

I see your shoddy craftsmanship

I feel the grime inside your throat

But hope for hollow equine threat

My programming, particular

My sensors finely tuned, too tightly

I fight against your attempts to rewrite me

As a flawlessly functional cyborg

Clamouring for love,

For the social conditioning

I nod more convincingly

To keep them from advancing

But you can't stop progress

And progress is exciting.

When You're Ten Years Ago

I was twenty-two before I let someone get close

You weren't always nice

And I wasn't always easy

I didn't know yet

How to process or how to grieve

Without being cruel

And when I couldn't articulate

How loss felt

I'd pitch coffee mugs at my back fence

Just to know something was broken

It was sort of this tragic cemetery

Where good cups went to die

But I needed you to know

My hurt was so great

That a girl who talks like white water

Had nothing but a kicked dog in her throat.

Reverb

I have this little rage in me
I build more stamina every day
To hold it down, to
Resist engaging

I feel blood burn
Through wool and leather

Healthy cells get attacked sometimes
There was nothing wrong with me

You defend me like a lion
As you puncture my skin

I don't think you can see it from here
I don't think it sounds the same to you

I pull out the cord
Put it safe in a room
My eyes remain focussed
And I feel bulletproof.

Royal

One old guy speaks to some old guy
Standing by a fire
Another one down in a wedding gown
Are you sleeping here tonight?

One old guy, shaking head
Left, right
Face flat like a tyre
Empire rose just to spit on folks
Another night spent by a fire

Talkin' bout headlines
Yeah, headlines
Not lines spent waiting in the rain
Some folks dying over girl in white
And some folks doing just the same.

A Forest in Suburbia

When I was a kid we lived in the pink house

With the wall of mirrors and the giant swan

I took a pair of gold-tipped hairdresser's scissors

And cut a hole, little by little

Through the thick pine needle hedge

Connecting our house & the one beside us

I kept on cutting

Till the hole was big enough

For me and Rhiannon from next door

To squeeze into a space in the middle

And when there were storms

We would meet up inside the hedge and talk about

What it must be like for kids in other cities

Where the sun's always out and the night winds

Come on slow like a waltz

And the houses are built from tree trunks

Thicker than blood.

Global and Gorecki

It's hard to live alone and it's hard to be loved
    Your bed feels too big, then it's **not big enough**
        And then you're hyper-aware of upsetting someone
Who just wants to adore you

        I wear your world over my ears when mine
      Gets deafening
    I remix your reverb, your warmth
You're **connective**.

I'm navigating conversations like open water
    It's the weight of the words
I measure them carefully but forget ingredients
    Occasionally
        And make a sinkhole out of it

      I'm getting better at paying attention
       Even when I really want to Google
        How to learn calculus in two days

Or how long it would take to walk
      From Perth to Adelaide
      Because I miss my little brother
          And plane tickets are expensive

But I find a filing cabinet up in my system
    And store the title of the book you've
      Just told me you've been trying to find.

Sometimes I forget to ask how your day was

Or see if you're really OK

Because I'm in my own head,

Just trying to breathe at a rate that doesn't startle anyone

I spend a lot of time wanting to sleep

In the little space under my desk

And I'd stay there for a week

Saying nothing at all

Just to conserve *some*

Small part of myself…

Then I hear you laughing

In the toilet

Watching vines on YouTube

And I feel like you're my person, too.

Night Bus Dreaming

String of street lamps like a Mexican wave

Linear, still night glowing blues under gold suns

You're mourning a dynasty as I sweep the night

I feel the pointlessness of anger as it slips through my bones
Away and away with the week

These steepled rooftops and stone fronts distract me
Long enough to chew slowly on words rushing
To the lip of me

It's been awhile but I have this little window
And I'm in no hurry to feel my boots kick at the leaves
On the doorstep

Driving past bankrupt fast food chains going under

And graveyards where we used to eat

All these little nooks some kids will never see

It's not that tragic but they'll taste a world
I won't recognize

My feet lock in just to see the river running with me

I haven't been that close on my own in a while

Petrol and wood smoke thick in the air
Reminds me of Robert Street and the old place
Built in the 1920s and the mannequin floor lamp
And the Persian rugs and the stuffy little dining room
With the hamsters and I can't help but feel
A bit nostalgic

I can be silent and still in a late night shuttle
The concertina crumple of full-time human beings

Wedged into rain-streaked window boxes

Just wanting to be left alone to decompress

Their accordion legs.

Made in the USA
Monee, IL
09 September 2021